SECRETS OF THE ANIMAL WORLD

BATS
Ultrasonic Navigators

by Eulalia García
Illustrated by Gabriel Casadevall and Ali Garousi

Gareth Stevens Publishing
MILWAUKEE

For a free color catalog describing Gareth Stevens' list of high-quality books, call 1-800-542-2595 (USA) or 1-800-461-9120 (Canada). Gareth Stevens' Fax: (414) 225-0377.

The editor would like to extend special thanks to Jan W. Rafert, Curator of Primates and Small Mammals, Milwaukee County Zoo, Milwaukee, Wisconsin, for his kind and professional help with the information in this book.

— *To Evenn Moore, who loves bats.*

Library of Congress Cataloging-in-Publication Data

García, Eulalia.
    [Murciélago. English]
    Bats: ultrasonic navigators / by Eulalia García; illustrated by Gabriel Casadevall and Ali Garousi.
        p. cm. — (Secrets of the animal world)
    Includes bibliographical references (p.   ) and index.
    Filmography: p.
    Summary: Provides detailed information on the physical characteristics and behavior of bats.
    ISBN 0-8368-1394-4 (lib. bdg.)
    1. Bats—Juvenile literature. [1. Bats.] I. Casadevall, Gabriel, ill. II. Garousi, Ali, ill.
III. Title. IV. Series.
QL737.C5G2613 1996
599.4—dc20   95-45836

This North American edition first published in 1996 by
Gareth Stevens Publishing
1555 North RiverCenter Drive, Suite 201
Milwaukee, Wisconsin 53212 USA

This U.S. edition © 1996 by Gareth Stevens, Inc. Created with original © 1993 Ediciones Este, S.A., Barcelona, Spain. Additional end matter © 1996 by Gareth Stevens, Inc.

Series editor: Patricia Lantier-Sampon
Editorial assistants: Diane Laska, Rita Reitci, Derek Smith

Printed in the United States of America

1 2 3 4 5 6 7 8 9 99 98 97 96

Sense of hearing

Although bats have good eyesight, they rely more on high-pitched sounds to guide them. Many bats, like dolphins, use a type of echolocation system, producing ultrasounds that humans cannot hear. When these sounds strike an object, they rebound back to the bat, which picks them up on its large ears, like a radar system. This takes only a few tenths of a second, and it enables the bat to know what is around it. Most kinds of bats produce these sounds in the larynx, sending them out of the mouth or nose.

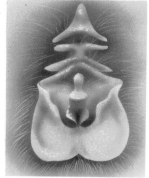

The strangely-shaped noses that many bats have allow them to send out very precise ultrasounds.

The bat's radar system helps it distinguish between prey and obstacles.

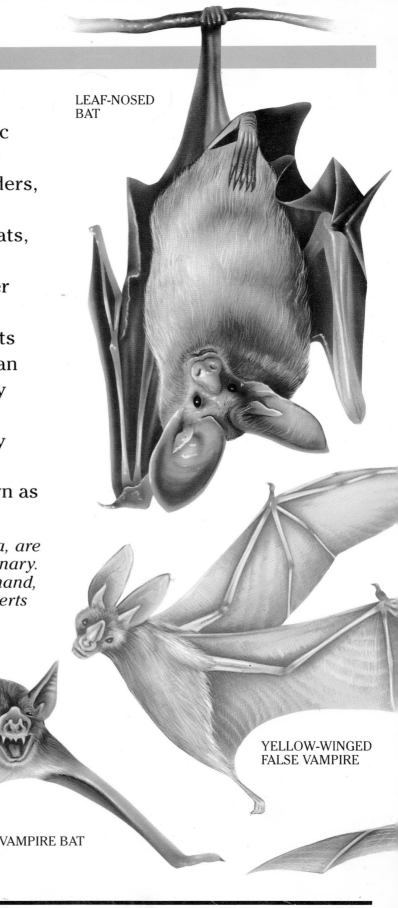

Wide variety of bats

Bats belong to the scientific order Chiroptera. The two main bat groups, or suborders, are Megachiroptera and Microchiroptera. Larger bats, with a 6.5-foot (2-meter) wingspan and a weight over 3 pounds (1.5 kg), are Megachiroptera. These bats have large eyes instead of an echolocation system. They most often find their food, mainly fruit and flowers, by using their eyes and nose. Megachiroptera, also known as

Flying foxes, or Megachiroptera, are large bats that look rather ordinary. Microchiroptera, on the other hand, look more sinister and are experts in producing ultrahigh sounds.

LEAF-NOSED BAT

YELLOW-WINGED FALSE VAMPIRE

VAMPIRE BAT

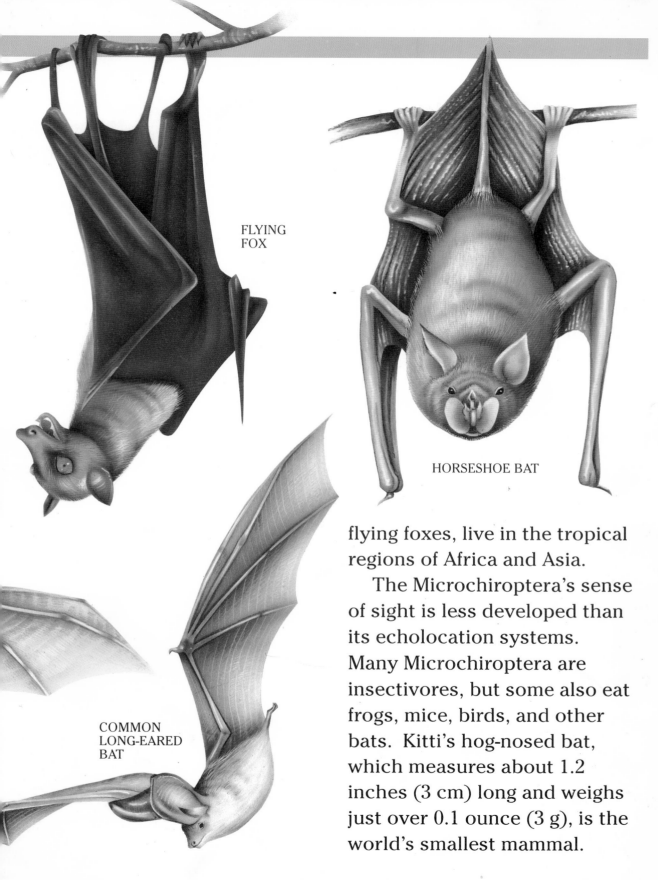

FLYING
FOX

HORSESHOE BAT

COMMON
LONG-EARED
BAT

flying foxes, live in the tropical regions of Africa and Asia.

The Microchiroptera's sense of sight is less developed than its echolocation systems. Many Microchiroptera are insectivores, but some also eat frogs, mice, birds, and other bats. Kitti's hog-nosed bat, which measures about 1.2 inches (3 cm) long and weighs just over 0.1 ounce (3 g), is the world's smallest mammal.

INSIDE THE BAT

Bats cannot fly as well as birds, although they have several other advantages. Their wings do not have feathers, and this sometimes causes dehydration. In spite of this, the bat's skeleton is strong and rigid, which enables it to fly and be guided by its radar in the dark.

BRAIN
The most developed part of the bat's brain keeps check on the outside world with radar. This is where echoes are received, located, and identified.

EARS
The bat's ears are large funnels that pick up the sound waves that rebound from objects. They can tell the bat whether a space is big enough to enter or not.

THUMB CLAW
All bats have thumb claws. These claws are used for climbing, swinging, scratching, holding food, and carrying young while in flight.

TRAGUS
A fleshy bulge that many bats have in the opening of the ear. Its function is to concentrate the sounds the ears pick up.

ESOPHAGU

NOSTRILS
The twisted shape of the nasal tubes can widen to pass sounds from the larynx. The nostrils direct the sound waves outward.

TEETH
Meat- and insect-eating bats have sharp, jagged teeth for chewing prey.

LARYNX
An organ that produces ultra-sounds for guiding the bat. The bat makes these sounds continually to stay aware of its surroundings.

TRACHEA

STERNUM
Bats possess many similarities to birds: one of them is the presence of a keel, or breastbone, in the sternum.

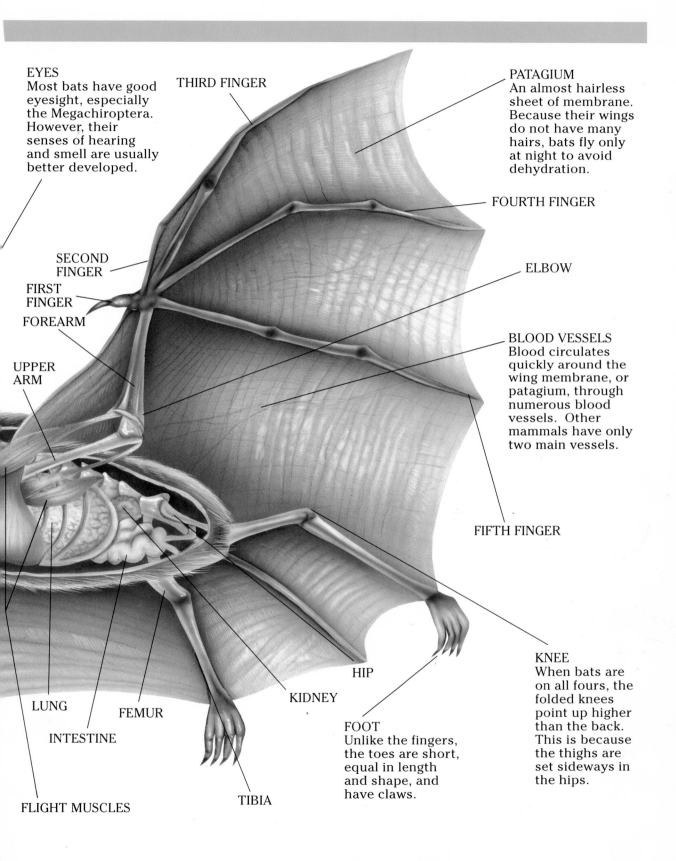

EYES
Most bats have good eyesight, especially the Megachiroptera. However, their senses of hearing and smell are usually better developed.

THIRD FINGER

PATAGIUM
An almost hairless sheet of membrane. Because their wings do not have many hairs, bats fly only at night to avoid dehydration.

FOURTH FINGER

SECOND FINGER

FIRST FINGER

FOREARM

ELBOW

UPPER ARM

BLOOD VESSELS
Blood circulates quickly around the wing membrane, or patagium, through numerous blood vessels. Other mammals have only two main vessels.

FIFTH FINGER

KNEE
When bats are on all fours, the folded knees point up higher than the back. This is because the thighs are set sideways in the hips.

HIP

KIDNEY

FOOT
Unlike the fingers, the toes are short, equal in length and shape, and have claws.

LUNG

FEMUR

INTESTINE

TIBIA

FLIGHT MUSCLES

THE BAT'S RADAR

Echoes in the dark

Bats produce ultrasounds — sounds of high frequency that humans cannot hear. These sounds are sent out through the mouth or nose. The nose is a maze of nooks and crannies. Some bats even have a nasal appendage that enables them to aim their ultrasounds in a specific direction. When these ultrasounds are sent out, they reflect from any object in their path in the form of an echo. The bat picks up these echoes with its enormous ears. The interior of the bat's ears are

The bat's ears receive echoes of its sound waves, which bounce off any body or object, in the same way radar detects aircraft.

To avoid being caught by bats, some moths can make sharp turns to confuse them. If a moth cannot escape this way, it drops down to hide in the undergrowth.

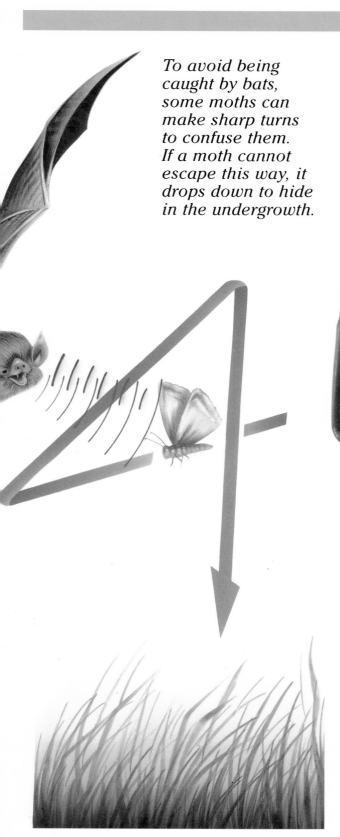

Special ear and nose structures in many bats pick up and emit ultrasounds (above). Other bats, with large eyes and small ears (left), guide themselves by sight and smell.

creased, and they contain an extra structure, called the tragus, that helps the bat concentrate the incoming echo.

Certain species of moths, the prey of many bats, recognize bat sounds. When they hear a bat nearby, they quickly move away. Some moths have even learned to imitate the bat's own sounds to disorient it. But many bats have also learned how to send their sounds on "another channel" to avoid this problem.

that young bats
go to kindergarten?

Most bats have only one baby a year. All births take place at the same time, and the young are placed together in caves. Each mother takes care of her own baby and no other.

She can recognize her offspring by its particular cry from far away, and its smell from nearby. Year after year, the female bats use the same caves to give birth and rear their young.

A complex system

The bat's complex radar system enables it to detect all objects, no matter how small. When an object vibrates, such as a leaf blowing in the wind, it produces sound waves that travel through the air. These sounds cannot be heard by humans.

When bats cry out, they become deaf so as not to hear themselves. This way, they only hear incoming echoes. They do not get confused, because they hear the sounds coming toward them, not what they send out.

When a bat becomes threatened, it produces a sound that the human ear can pick up, instead of its usual ultrasounds.

Bats make very high sounds that are transmitted in waves. When these waves hit an object or an animal, they rebound and are received by the bat's sharp ears, helping it identify its surroundings.

THE LIFE OF A BAT

Wings and flight

The bat's wings are made of thin, almost hairless elastic membrane with muscles, known as the patagium. It contains the long, thin finger bones. The patagium extends from the animal's body to the fingers, hind feet, and tail, although the tail is sometimes excluded.

The bat's radar system prevents it from colliding with obstacles in the air and within enclosed spaces. Bats fly in a crooked, twisting path when avoiding obstacles, but they can

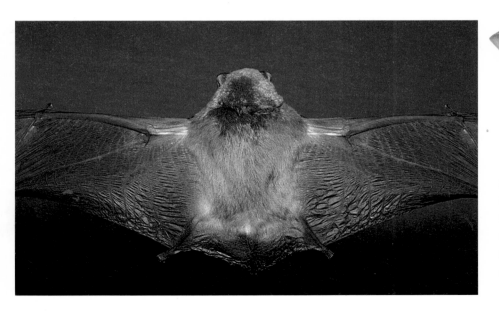

The bat's patagium is a flexible sheet of membrane and muscle. Its main function is to move the wings in flight.

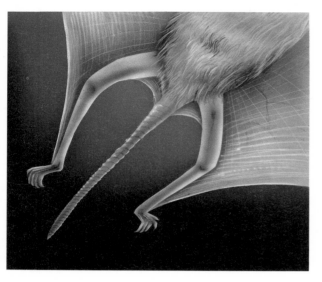

easily make rapid course changes. Every second, their ears receive hundreds of echoes that must be processed in the brain. The echolocation system quickly tells the bat how far away it is from an object by the amount of time the sounds take to travel and return.

There are two types of wings: narrow wings — useful for flying fast and typical of bats living in open spaces; and wide wings — useful for maneuvering slowly between tree branches and typical of bats living in crowded or enclosed areas.

Some bats have a tail as long as 2 inches (5 cm). In these cases, the tail is not included in the patagium. Instead, it hangs free.

Bats are expert fliers, even though they use ultrasounds instead of eyes.

that bats suck nectar?

Different bats consume insects, fruit, or blood, but some bats take nectar from flowers. These bats lap up nectar while hovering just above the blossom. Others settle on different flowers for a few minutes, and still others make sharp dives over them. To sip the nectar, bats use a tongue that is almost as long as their body. Bats, like bees, not only feed on flowers but also act as pollinators and help the flowers reproduce.

Living upside-down

Bats spend a lot of time hanging head downward. They can eat, wash, and sleep wrapped up in their wings in this position. Females give birth upside-down, and bats in temperate climates hibernate in this position.

The bat's foot has five toes of equal length, with strong claws at the end of

each, for hanging. This posture can be maintained because the foot tendons, when stretched out, will not allow the toes to straighten. The bat's arteries also have valves that keep the blood from rushing to its head.

The five toes of each hind foot of the bat easily support it while the bat hangs upside-down.

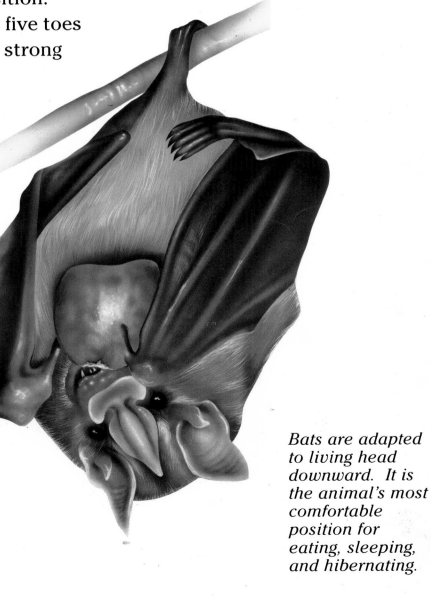

Bats are adapted to living head downward. It is the animal's most comfortable position for eating, sleeping, and hibernating.

ANCESTOR OF THE BAT

The first bat

Very little is known about the evolution of bats. The only fossils discovered date back just 55 million years, when the bat already evolved its present appearance. Its ability to "see" in the dark by producing ultrasounds depended on the development of the bat's larynx, ears, nose, and brain. The first bat, Icaronycteris, lived in North America. Its wings were short and wide, and its long tail was not connected to the

Icaronycteris was very similar to most modern bats, except that it had two sharp claws instead of only one.

patagium. Two of the bat's five fingers carried claws — on the thumb and the index finger. Icaronycteris hunted insects at night to avoid enemy birds.

The first known bat fossil was Icaronycteris, which had the capacity to "see," using ultrasounds.

Did **YOU** **?Know** ...

that bats are excellent crawlers and leapers?

Although bats normally hang upside-down or fly, they can walk and even hop along the ground. A bat's body has a peculiar feature: its legs stick out sideways from its body. When the legs bend at the hip, the knees fold up above the bat's back. A bat rests on the ground by using its wrists and feet as support, keeping its wings folded over its back.

Wing functions

A bat hanging head down wraps its wings around itself for warmth. Bats that hang from tree branches also cover themselves with the patagium or use it like a fan in hot weather. The wing patagium enables the bat to catch prey easily, and the tail patagium holds the food until the bat can hang upside-down to eat. Some female bats often hang upside-down to give birth, catching the newborn in the patagium.

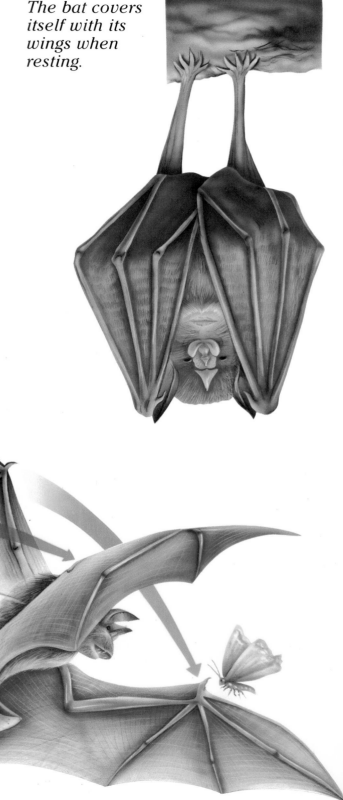

The bat covers itself with its wings when resting.

The bat's wings can trap flying insects.

THE BEHAVIOR OF BATS

Vampire bats

The vampire bat rarely attacks humans. Its main victims are horses, pigs, cows, and mules. It is only found in the tropics and subtropics of America, where farmers are also afraid it infects their livestock with rabies. When the vampire bat finds its prey, it scuttles on its wrists and feet around the animal until it finds an area of uncovered flesh. The bat then bites the victim with its sharp incisors. Blood flows from wound and is lapped up on the bat's tongue. The bat's saliva contains an anticoagulant to keep the blood from clotting.

The vampire bat's tongue folds in at the sides to form a channel that, with the furrow of the lower lip, carries the blood into its mouth.

Vampire bats can consume 40 percent of their body weight in blood, in sessions of 8-18 minutes.

Hibernation

Some animals, such as bears and squirrels, hibernate to conserve energy. But no animal can lower its body temperature like the boreal red bat, whose temperature during hibernation drops to as low as 23°F (-5°C).

In summer heat, many bats become lethargic and breathe only every three to eight minutes. As the day cools, they breathe about twenty-five to thirty times a minute. When bats are very active, they may breathe over two hundred times a minute.

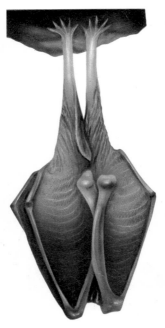

Bats conserve energy during hibernation (left) by insulating themselves and lowering their body temperature.

The bat's skin swells and dampens (right) as a result of cave humidity when its body temperature drops.

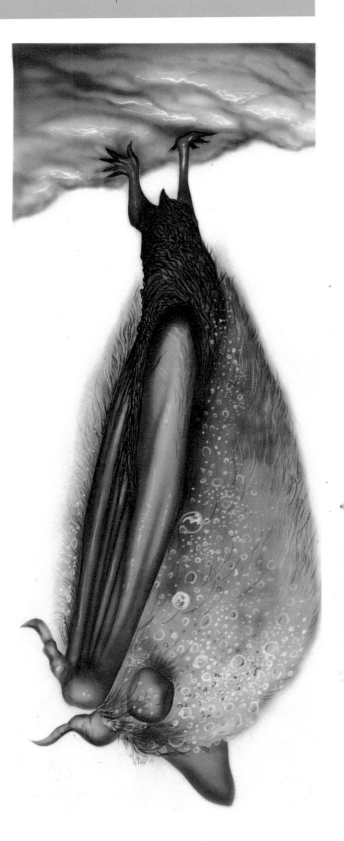

Fisher bats

The fisher bats feed on fish they catch in the waters of tropical America. The fisher bats locate their prey using echolocation. They also fly slowly over the water's surface with their feet submerged. Their wings are taut and the skin impermeable, so they rarely get wet during these random sweeps over the water. Fisher bats can catch up to thirty or forty small fish each night. The bats tear the fish into pieces and carry them in their enormous cheek bags to chew later on.

Certain fish leap out of the water and grab bats to eat.

Fisher bats have to be careful when hunting, however, because many fish try to capture the bats by leaping out of the water to grab them.

The fisher bat does not get wet when it sweeps the surface of the water.

APPENDIX TO

SECRETS
OF THE
ANIMAL WORLD

BATS
Ultrasonic Navigators

BAT SECRETS

Good fertilizer. Some bats live in caves. Guano, or excrement, from these caves is a valuable fertilizer.

▼ White bats. White bats, known as ghost bats, live in the tropical regions of America. These bats are not albinos.

▼ Hammerhead bat. This bat's name comes from the male's unusual hammer-shaped head, which includes two inflatable bags and an enormous larynx.

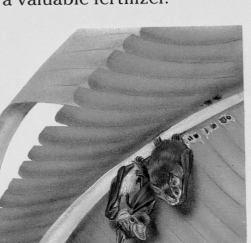

▲ Construction bats. These bats build cabins from palm leaves, folding them along the vein. The cabins protect the bats from enemies and poor weather.

▼ Clinging to the mother.
Some female bats have an extra pair of breasts in the groin area that do not secrete milk. When the offspring fly along with their mother, they cling to these dry breasts with their hooked milk teeth.

Getting a jump start. Some people claim that, even in hibernation, bats remain alert in case any predators approach them. In such cases, they can rapidly speed up their metabolism, raise their temperature, and escape.

1. What is a tragus and where is it?
a) An appendage in the hind legs, for scratching.
b) An fleshy bulge in the ears to concentrate echoes.
c) A labyrinth in the nose for producing ultrahigh sounds.

2. The wings of the bats are used for:
a) keeping warm, hunting, and flying.
b) flying, fishing, and producing ultrasounds.
c) refreshing themselves and picking up echoes.

3. Vampire bats mainly bite:
a) humans.
b) livestock.
c) insectivores.

4. Why are bats nocturnal animals?
a) They would dehydrate during the daytime.
b) They see better at night.
c) It is not so hot at night.

5. When bats hibernate,:
a) they stretch out on the floor.
b) they increase their heartbeat.
c) their body temperature drops.

The answers to BAT SECRETS questions are on page 32.

GLOSSARY

anticoagulant: a substance that prevents blood from clotting. A vampire bat's saliva contains an anticoagulant to keep its victim's wound open and the blood from clotting.

appendages: body parts that are not parts of the main body, such as limbs. A bat's legs and wings are appendages.

arteries: tubes inside the body that carry blood from the heart to all areas of the body. Bats' arteries have special valves that prevent blood from rushing to the head when the animals hang upside-down.

dehydration: the process in which water leaves or is removed from something. The wings of a bat are vulnerable to dehydration because there is no protective covering to keep moisture in. When bats fly, the air can dry out their wings.

disoriented: confused. Because bats rely on their radar system to navigate, anything that interferes with this can cause them to become disoriented and lose their way.

echolocation: also called a bat's "radar," this is how a bat navigates. Bats send out sounds that bounce, or echo, off the bat's surroundings. This gives them a sound-picture of their location, distance from objects, and the size of their prey.

evolution: the process of changing shape or developing gradually over time. All living things change and adapt to survive or they can become extinct. Scientists learn more about how organisms develop by studying how they once were or what their ancestors were like through fossils.

femur: of a bat's two leg segments, this one is closest to the body.

hibernation: a state of inactivity in which most body functions, such as heartbeat and breathing, slow down. Some bat species hibernate during winter months to survive the freezing temperatures.

hovering: staying suspended in the same place while in the air.

impermeable: a covering or material that does not let substances, such as water, pass through it. The fisher bat is able to stay dry when it hunts for fish because its skin is impermeable.

incisors: sharp teeth used for cutting into food. A vampire bat has very sharp incisors that it uses to bite a victim and feed.

insectivores: creatures that eat only insects.

labyrinth: a maze with many passages, twists, and turns.

larynx: the voice organ that contains the vocal cords. In humans, this is where the voice originates. In bats, this is where ultrasounds are created.

lethargic: sluggish, slowed down.

Megachiroptera: one of the two main scientific groups of bats. Bats belonging to this group, known commonly as flying foxes, are much larger than the bats belonging to the other group, Microchiroptera.

membrane: a thin, soft, flexible layer or covering.

Microchiroptera: one of the two main scientific groups of bats. These bats are smaller than those belonging to the group Megachiroptera. The Microchiroptera rely on echolocation to navigate.

nocturnal: active primarily at night. Bats are nocturnal.

nurse: to produce milk to feed young; to drink the milk produced by a female mammal's body.

patagium: the scientific name for a bat's wings. The wings are made of membrane and muscle.

pollinators: agents in the fertilization of flowers that act by carrying the pollen from one flower to another. Fruit bats are pollinators, much like bees, as they travel from flower to flower while feeding on nectar.

radar: something that emits

waves to determine distance, the size of an object, or an object's speed. While radar is commonly thought of as a humanmade invention, bats use a similar system that is natural. A bat's radar is known as echolocation.

reproduce: to create offspring and bear young.

tendon: a tough cord or band of tissue that connects muscle to bone.

tibia: of the two leg sections in a bat, this one connects the femur to the foot.

trachea: the main breathing tube that carries air into the lungs.

ultrasounds: sounds that humans cannot hear. Bats produce these high-frequency sound waves as part of their radar navigation system, or echolocation.

ACTIVITIES

◆ Find out more about echolocation and radar. Bats have a unique method of navigating and sensing their surroundings. Compare how a bat "sees" with how a dolphin, lion, ant, and human see. Learn more about humanmade radar, too. What materials are they made of, and how are they constructed? Under what conditions do they work best? Do they work in the same way as the bat's radar?

◆ Many species of bats are endangered. Contrary to popular myth, they are not the threat and nuisance to humans, livestock, and fruit orchards they are often accused of. Write to the following organization to find out which bats are endangered and what you can do to help save them. Getting involved with a conservation effort can be a rewarding experience, both for you and bats!

Bat Conservation International
P.O. Box 162603
Austin, TX 78716-2603

MORE BOOKS TO READ

Amazing Bats. Frank Greenaway (Knopf)
Batman: Exploring the World of Bats. Laurence Pringle (Scribners)
The Bat in the Cave. Helen Riley (Gareth Stevens)
Bats. (Creative Education)
Bats. Michael George (Child's World)
Bats. Sharon S. Shebar and Susan E. Shebar (Watts)
Bats: A Nature-Fact Book. D. J. Arneson (Kidsbooks)
Bats. Let's Read and Find Out about Science Series. Ann Earle
    (HarperCollins)
Extremely Weird Bats. Sarah Lovett (John Muir)
Flyers. John B. Wexo (Troll Associates)
Shadows of the Night: The Hidden World of the Little Brown Bat.
    Barbara Bash (Sierra)
Those Amazing Bats. Cheryl M. Halton (Macmillan)

VIDEOS

Bats. (Bullfrog Films, Inc.)
The Bats of Carlsbad. (National AudioVisual Center)
Vampire. (Films, Inc. Video)

PLACES TO VISIT

**Metropolitan Toronto
    Zoo**
Meadowvale Road
West Hill
Toronto, Ontario
M1E 4R5

Bronx Zoo
185th Street and
    Southern Boulevard
Bronx, NY 10460

Granby Zoo
347 Bourget Street
Granby, Quebec
J2G 1E8

Taronga Zoo
Bradleys Head Road
Mosman, New South
    Wales
Australia 2088

Otago Museum
419 Great King Street
Dunedin, New Zealand

Brookfield Zoo
First Avenue and
    31st Street
Brookfield, IL 60513

INDEX

Answers to BAT SECRETS questions:
1. **b**
2. **a**
3. **b**
4. **a**
5. **c**